Welcome to Our Church

A Handbook for Greeters and Ushers

Everything should be done
in a fitting and orderly way.

(1 Corinthians 14:40)

Annette Schroeder

CPH.
SAINT LOUIS

This booklet is designed for self-study
by greeters and ushers, new or experienced.

It can also be used for group study.

In a Nutshell:

What visitors want and don't want

- To be noticed but not spotlighted.
- To be treated respectfully and greeted warmly (children and teenagers too).
- To be listened to warmly, not talked at.
- To be given any guidance needed to participate in the service.
- To meet the pastor, if possible.
- To meet other people similar to themselves.
- To have his/her name remembered.
- To have questions answered (where to park; times of the services; when there is Bible study; where rest rooms are; if there are activities or provisions for their children [such as a nursery] and teens; etc.).
- Not to be bombarded with a hard-sell approach to membership in the church, or even for repeat visits.

A greeter/usher must

- Act as the host to visitors as a representative of the whole congregation. May be a single adult, teenager, couple, or an entire family.
- Be neatly dressed and wearing a greeter or usher name badge and boutonniere, if provided.
- Be there well before the service begins.
- Smile with genuine warmth and offer a handshake to visitors.
- Be hospitable and outgoing.
- Listen to a visitor's wants and needs.

- Be trained.
- Participate in the worship service. Each greeter and usher needs a hymnal and worship folder to use during the service. Greeters may be seated in the congregation 10 or 15 minutes into the service.
- Not be expected to be a greeter every Sunday, but at intervals.
- Find a substitute if he/she cannot be present.

An usher must

- Hand out bulletins/worship folders/etc., and provide a word of explanation if needed.
- Be attentive to people and pastor every moment, in case of a need or an emergency.
- Responsible for unlocking doors, turning on/off lights, opening/closing windows, adjusting heating/air conditioning, turning on/off sound system.
- Mark any reserved seating (such as back rows for parents with small children) and guide those who are to sit there to seats in that section.
- Encourage people to sit toward the front of the nave.
- Be sensitive to and assist those who have disabilities and need special help: hard-of-hearing or deaf, blind, elderly, in wheelchairs, etc.
- Maintain a quiet atmosphere in the narthex when the service begins.
- Turn on the speaker in the nursery so the caretakers can hear the worship service, if applicable.
- Count the worshipers unobtrusively.
- Gather the offering; take it to the altar and know where and how long to stand before the altar.

- Assist with Holy Communion: direct the worshipers smoothly and quickly. Help those with any difficulties. Gather communion registration cards, if applicable.
- Assist with Holy Baptism.
- Set out the guest book and pen or direct guests to sign visitor cards; put offering plates in place; post hymn numbers; check emergency supplies (such as first-aid kit); etc.
- Check supplies in the ushers' cabinet/closet and order those supplies that run low or have run out.

Contents

I. GREETERS

Introduction: Greeters as Hosts

Mrs. S. visited a Lutheran church in San Diego, California, while she was vacationing there. Not one person in the congregation spoke to her—including the ushers! She felt like an outsider or an intruder.

A few months later, while visiting relatives in Wisconsin, Mrs. S. went to a Lutheran church in Milwaukee one Sunday morning. This time, someone pinned a "visitor" badge on her, but it didn't seem to mean anything to members or ushers—or even the pastor! She was angry enough to write a letter to the church. She told them: "If I were moving into your area, I would definitely not join your congregation. You care nothing about visitors."

She never heard from the congregation or the pastor, but maybe her letter prompted a greeter movement in their church.

Perhaps Mrs. S. is more sensitive about being greeted in a new church because she is on the greeter committee at her home church. She doubts that. Everyone wants to feel welcome—whether at someone's home or someone's church. If you don't feel welcome, you are uncomfortable the whole time you're there and you don't want to come back.

Greeters are the hosts for God's house—the doorkeepers who serve those who enter His house. Remember Psalm 84:10: "I would rather be a doorkeeper in the house of my God than dwell in the tents of the wicked."

What is a greeter? usher?

In this booklet, a *greeter* is an outgoing, friendly church member (of any age) who greets visitors at the church door and makes them feel welcome.

In this booklet, an *usher* is an outgoing, friendly person who assists in seeing that the service runs smoothly and as planned.

Who are the greeters?

In a small congregation, ushers may also be the greeters. In a larger congregation, ushers and greeters should be separate groups. Separate is best since each has different responsibilities to do before the worship service begins.

Ideally, congregation members volunteer as greeters in response to a request to fill the need as expressed by the greeter committee, a committee under the evangelism board or the board of elders. Committee members should call possible greeters or ask them in person if they would serve as greeters once or twice a month at one of the Sunday services. Those recruited should be friendly and outgoing people.

Greeters can be singles, couples, teenagers, or entire families. They can be elderly or young—as long as they can smile and shake hands.

White tie and tails?

To be a greeter, formal dress isn't necessary; casual dress isn't appropriate. Just dress neatly in clothes appropriate to attending church. You don't want your appearance to shock the visitors.

What might be inappropriate to wear? One greeter wore a Santa Claus cap to greet people during Advent, making the season seem secular and comical instead of a celebration of Christ's coming. Several worshipers complained to the pastor that the Santa Claus cap was inappropriate in a church setting. It was not seen again.

Arrive at least 20 minutes before the service begins; you should be there to greet even the earliest worshipers. Wear a name tag that is readable from a distance—and a boutonniere, if one is provided.

Say a prayer before you begin. Ask God to help you greet everyone as if you were Christ's representative. (You are!)

Smile! Smile! Smile!

How can you spot a visitor?

Recognizing visitors may be difficult, if you aren't familiar with all the church members.

- Search for people who look tentative or lost or unsure of where to go.
- Look for people you don't recognize. Better to ask than to overlook a visitor.

- _____
- _____

How can visitors recognize you as a greeter?

- By the fact that you are looking and smiling at the people who enter the church.
- By your appearance: _____
- _____

A name tag, a card, or a guest book?

Encourage your congregation to supply visitor name tags. Ask every visitor to write his or her name with a bright, bold marking pen and wear the tag before, during, and after the service. That way, the pastor and the members know for sure who is visiting so they can greet them.

Also, ask each visitor to sign the guest book or hand them a visitor card to fill out. It is important! Then the church has a record of who was visiting for follow-up calls.

A name tag helps people identify visitors during the time they visit. However, a visitor card or a guest book will give the information needed to follow up on the guests later.

A warning!

A retired pastor and his wife visited another church. They encountered three separate sets of greeters before they got to the nave (the part of a church building where the worshipers sit). He said it "turned them off" as much as if they had not been welcomed at all.

The welcoming can be overdone. Don't lavish so much attention on visitors that it overwhelms them.

How much attention is too much? Determining that comes with experience, but take your cue from the visitors themselves. If they don't return your greeting, let them pass. Don't keep after them. You can overdo the greeting thing.

A simple way to prevent this is by giving them a visitor name tag to wear. If the visitors have tags, they have already been greeted and need only a smile from other members.

Option: The visitor's booth

If you have room at the doorway, you might set up a table with a sign above it saying "Information." The sign should be high enough to be seen over the crowd. Place the table and sign where the people enter from the parking lot.

Two greeters plus an escort or two could be at the information table 15 or 20 minutes before the service. The table might display some printed information about the church and its programs. Greeters at the table should hand out the information and offer to answer any questions the visitors have.

If an information packet has been prepared and as you have time, show each visitor what is inside the packet—especially the floor plan that shows them where things are located in the building.

Another way to guide visitors to the right places in the building is to use escorts. Escorts may show visitors the way to the nave where they may be put into the care of other greeters or ushers. Some escorts should be ready to take children to other parts of the building for their own worship service or for Sunday school. Some can escort parents with small children to the nursery.

The Greeter from the Visitor's Point of View

To really understand what you are expected to do as a greeter, think about how the visitor might see you and the congregation.

How important is a greeter?

For a long time, Mr. and Mrs. J. K. wanted to try going to their neighborhood church. When they finally made it there, the assigned greeter couple for that Sunday forgot they were to come early. With no one to make them feel welcome, Mr. and Mrs. J. K. never came back—even though they lived just around the corner. They signed the guest book. As a greeter, how might you win them back?

You, the greeter, are the first impression any visitor has of the people in your congregation. If you are at your Sunday morning post and are friendly and helpful, the visitor will probably assume the other people in the congregation are friendly and helpful too.

Think of how important you are as a greeter by trying to see yourself from the visitor's point of view. Concentrate on how the visitor will see you. Will his or her first impression be a favorable one? Will you make the person very glad he or she came to your church? (We will return to this topic below.)

In addition, people have judged a church—rightly or wrongly—by the services and programs it offers. People are attracted by a church that is sensitive to their needs: preschool, active youth group, single or older adult ministry, day care—even the kind of music used in services—and so on. Therefore, they will judge the church by how it treats *them*. Are they valued or just tolerated? You, as a greeter, may be the reason they come back.

But, to a visitor, warmth, genuine friendliness, and caring are still the most important qualities of a church. Visitors need more than a parking space and a bulletin.

Yes, they expect more genuine warmth and friendliness from church members than from the people they encounter in the world. Visitors expect church members to be obviously different than other people. The church members' joy in the Lord must be evident on their faces and must radiate to visitors.

A greeter forges the visitor's first link to the congregation. How strong that link is will be determined by how the greeter behaves toward the visitor from the first moment they meet.

Imagine ...

Split yourself into two people for a moment. Imagine yourself in the place of a visitor to your church encountering yourself as one of the greeters that day.

What three positive traits would you as a visitor notice about you, a greeter?

_____

What one or two negative traits might you as a visitor notice?

_____

How would you feel as a first-time visitor to your church if you were the greeter? What would you notice first about the people?

_____

_____

How might your personal positive traits attract a visitor?

_____

_____

How might your negative trait(s) repel a visitor?

_____

_____

What can you do to overcome your negative trait(s) and emphasize your positive trait(s)?_____

_____

What would you, as a visitor, expect from a greeter? What would you hope the greeter would *not* do? The next section should help you consider these questions.

What visitors want (and don't want) from greeters

Most visitors want to be noticed but not spotlighted. Making a great fuss over visitors or asking them to stand during the service is spotlighting them. (Anything that makes visitors feel uncomfortable should be avoided.) Smiling, welcoming, shaking hands, asking their names one-on-one is noticing them.

Visitors want to be greeted warmly (children and teenagers too) and treated respectfully. To decide how to do this, think first how you would feel in the visitors' place. If there is a Sunday school or children's worship service scheduled, tell parents and children what it is, when and where. Have escorts ready for the children— unless the parents would prefer to escort their children themselves.

One thing visitors *don't* want from greeters is a hard-sell approach to membership in the church, or even for repeat visits. Greeters need to ask if visitors have any questions about the church and then answer them. Greeters need to refer visitors to the pastor if their questions are theological (about the church's teachings). The pastor needs to greet all visitors as he does all members before or after the service.

Beyond answering their questions, do not ask the visitors for any kind of commitment to the church—not even for repeat visits. The greeters can say, "We are glad to have you worship with us today. Please come again soon." Anything more than this is inappropriate and may even embarrass your guests.

A Chinese teenager, who was attending a Christian church service for the first time, asked a teenage church member: "How do you become a member of this church?" When the host teenager told the Chinese teen that Baptism would make her a member of the church, she asked what Baptism was. The answering teen was overwhelmed, so she asked an adult church member to help with the explanations. It turned out that the Chinese girl was simply curious, not looking for a way to join the church. However, how might the host teen follow up on the Chinese girl? Identify several ways and write them here:

_____

_____

_____

_____

Be practical!

Give the visitor information about the church that might be needed (or direct them to someone who can provide the information). To inform visitors, you need to be familiar with the church building, the church staff, and the programs offered by your congregation. If the visitors express a particular interest, such as adult Bible study, you can introduce them to the Bible study teacher or a member of one of the classes. That way, they will already know someone in the class when they go to the Bible class.

Give visitors practical information or have someone standing by to give information: where the nave is (if not obvious), where rest rooms are, where the nursery is (if they have children with them), where the fellowship hall is (if a fellowship time follows the service), where and when Sunday school and/or Bible classes are held.

If your congregation has prepared a brochure or an information packet for visitors, be sure each visitor (or family) receives one. Offer to answer any questions he or she may have. Be certain the information contains the church's complete phone number in a conspicuous place so the visitors can have questions answered even after they return home.

Update the information packet frequently so that the contents are current. If there is a summer vacation Bible school, for example, be sure a flyer giving dates and times is included in the late-winter and early-spring visitor packets.

What might an information packet for your congregation include? Make a list and give your list to the evangelism committee for consideration.

1. _____
2. _____
3. _____
4. _____
5. _____

How can you give the visitor too much information? What might "too much" include?

Remember the name!

It may seem unimportant, but people like it when you remember their name. Ask for it when you greet them. Ask them to repeat it or spell it. You repeat it too. Then do whatever you can to remember that name.

- Write it down and read the name(s) over and over.
- Collect the filled-out visitor cards.
- Check the guest book after they sign.
- Use a memory device—such as a rhyming word ("sweeter Peter") or an image (an egg in a tiny cart for "Eckart") to recall the name.
- _____
- _____

After the service, bid farewell *by name* to as many of the visitors as you can. Say something like: "Mr. and

Mrs. Miller, we enjoyed having you with us. Please come again."

Teens will be especially impressed if you remember their names. Say, "Goodbye, James (or Jane). I hope you come back soon to worship with us." Introducing the visiting teen to a teen church member or the youth minister gives the visitor the impression that you really care about him or her.

Also, children appreciate being noticed. Adults always seem to be shaking hands above their heads. Bend or squat to the child visitor's level and ask the child to give his or her own name. Use it when addressing something to the child, such as, "Susie (or Sammy), we have a children's worship service (or Sunday school) that is just for you. Would you like to try it once?"

Jesus said, "Whoever welcomes a little child like this in My name welcomes Me" (Matthew 18:5).

A Greeter's Attitude

A trade secret: The acceptance mode

Imagine this scenario: It is Sunday morning. Everything has gone wrong for you. The toast burned. You spilled coffee on your clothes and had to change them. Your hair just wouldn't behave. Your car wouldn't start. You are late. You assume your role as a greeter just a few minutes before the service, but you are angry and upset. You stand in your place with your arms crossed. You are definitely not smiling. The best you can do is nod toward people.

If this were you, what would you do about how you feel at that moment? How are you jeopardizing your greeting? How can you make the sun come out for you and for the people you greet? How could Psalm 33 (or another psalm) help you?

It's so important to be in an accepting mood (or mode) when you are a greeter. It's not always easy to do, but the secret is to *focus on the visitor and not on yourself.*

If you refocus your attention onto the visitor, you will find you are unfolding your arms, leaning forward, listening carefully, and smiling warmly as you reach out with an invitation to shake hands. Your body language says volumes of caring before you have even opened your mouth. By the time you speak to a visitor, he or she is probably already smiling back and may have shaken the hand you offered.

The rest of your job is much easier if you are in an acceptance mode—and not just pretending to be. Your whole presentation—body and words—will tell the visitors you are glad to see them and want to help them.

Think for a moment: Which stores do you go back to and shop in? Isn't it usually the stores where an associate seemed genuinely helpful and friendly, and who wasn't just going through the motions of being helpful?

Doctors who have kind, caring nurses will have much calmer patients in their examining rooms. The same is true of dentist offices—or of anywhere you go where you might have some anxiety about going.

The acceptance mode will pull visitors in and will bring them back. Sometimes, however, acceptance is difficult. What might make acceptance of visitors difficult for you? Consider the example in the next section.

This is a tough one!

Someone has said that you haven't been ignored until you've been ignored by a cat. Strangely, however, even when a cat is deliberately ignoring you, she will turn her ears toward your voice. She's still listening and is aware of you. Human beings could take a pay-attention lesson from cats! Listen! Listen, even when you don't want to listen.

Consider this: Suppose a teenager—a girl—came into your church building just before worship time, and you are the greeter that day. The girl is dressed in the teen "uniform": oversize shirt, faded jeans, clunky shoes. What's more, her grown-out bangs hide much of her face. She stops near you and just stands there while you greet a lovely family and make sure they know where things are. You are so busy with the visiting family that you don't notice the teenage girl. She pushes back the hair from her face and tries to catch your eyes with hers. She attempts to speak to you, but you just keep talking to the family. To you, the girl is invisible.

After several minutes, the girl gives up and turns to leave the building. You finally notice her—as she is walking away. What can you do at that moment to bring her back and make her feel accepted? Or, would you even want to? Explain why you might not want to.

Here's an important thought: Did you ignore the girl because she was different than you (Be honest!)? Or, maybe you thought she couldn't possibly be a visitor. She looked so—well, strange, out of place, inappropriately dressed.

"And you are to love those who are aliens" (Deuteronomy 10:19). No matter how difficult it is for you to overcome your feelings about her appearance, she is still a guest in the Lord's house. The Holy Spirit invited her to come to church. Who are you to ignore God's invited guest?

Instead, greet the teenage girl as warmly as you would greet anyone else. Be sure to get her name. Ask if she has any questions. Listen carefully to her and answer promptly and respectfully.

One thing this visitor especially needs is a second link to the congregation (after you). Your best bet is to beckon to a teenage church member (or have one standing by) and introduce your teenage visitor to that teen *by name*. That person can become the teen visitor's escort to the worship area or youth Bible class and can stay with the teen visitor to act as guide and mentor. The teen escort can introduce the teen visitor to other teens and can be sure the teen visitor is invited back to worship, Bible study, or teen activities.

God's Word speaks on "attitude"

Read Galatians 5:22–25. How does a Christian in the role of greeter or usher demonstrate each "fruit of the Spirit"? (A suggested answer is given, but you may wish to discuss these Christian attributes further.)

Love: It is an attitude about people that reaches out with concern for them and their needs (not your own needs). The Bible says, "The alien living with you must be treated as one of your native-born. Love him as yourself" (Leviticus 19:34).

Can you love someone you just met? God loves him or her, but can you honestly love a person "at first sight"?

Joy: With the Holy Spirit's help, can you put your heart into your greeter/usher duties so they don't become a mechanical chore? Joy should show on your facc and be a permanent state of mind. Is "joyful" the same as "cheerful"?

"The LORD is my strength and my shield; my heart trusts in Him, and I am helped. My heart leaps for joy and I will give thanks to Him in song" (Psalm 28:7). What is the secret of feeling joyful?

Peace: Keep calm no matter what happens, and keep peaceful order in the worship service. How can you do that even when there is a disturbance or an emergency?

When the pastor blesses the congregation with "the peace of God, which transcends all understanding" (Philippians 4:7), what is meant by "peace"? Why isn't it just the absence of conflict?

Patience: Don't allow people to make you "lose your cool" (which is easier said than done). The calmer you are when you deal with problems, for example, the less disruptive they will be. Also, waiting for people—which takes patience—is hard to do calmly, especially in a church setting. Name two synonyms for patience. Can you think of situations where patience is necessary for ushers and greeters?

Kindness: Pay attention to the needs of others and see their needs as opportunities to help and show love. How does that translate to the worship setting?

Goodness: The Holy Spirit can give you a heart that is good—that seeks what is good for those around you—at home, at work, and at church. How can you tell when someone has God's goodness in his or her heart?

Faithfulness: *Responsible* and *trustworthy* are two synonyms for "faithful." For what tasks can the pastor and the people depend on you?

Gentleness: Deal with a disruptive child as gently as you would anyone else. A quiet voice and a gentle touch will be effective. Whom do you know that can be described as gentle?

Self-control: Even if everything goes wrong, stay calm and clearheaded. If you want to control a large group of people, you have to be in control of yourself. What happens when you lose your self-control?

After you have considered/discussed how each "fruit of the Spirit" applies to you as a greeter/usher, underline the one or two you need to work on most. Pray for each spiritual gift, especially for the one(s) you are weakest in. Ask for a special measure of the Holy Spirit to overcome your weaknesses in attitude.

Never forget for a moment that you are not the boss (even if you are the head usher); you are a servant to Christ and to His people—an attendant. And the servant role usually calls for an attitude adjustment. On this scale, rate your current attitude toward your servant role as greeter/usher. What might you be able to do to improve your attitude?

SELF-CENTERED ——————— OTHER-CENTERED

Do nothing out of selfish ambition or vain conceit, but in humility consider others better than yourselves. Each of you should look not only to your own interests, but also to the interest of others. Your attitude should be the same as that of Christ Jesus: Who, being in very nature God, did not consider equality with God something to be grasped, but made Himself nothing, taking the very nature of a servant, being made in human likeness. And being found in appearance as a man, He humbled Himself and became obedient to death—even death on a cross!

(Philippians 2:3–8)

Just what does it mean to be a servant, an attendant, especially in a church setting? How is Jesus' attitude an example for your own attitude adjustment?

Also, what is humility? How is humility necessary for the role of greeter/usher? Read John 13:2–17. How is this a model of humility? How does it help you to understand your servant role as greeter/usher?

As a greeter/usher servant, watch carefully during the service to quickly solve problems that arise—not because you are "in charge," but because you do not want the worship or the worshipers disturbed.

Welcome the members too!

Not only are greeters to welcome guests, greeters should welcome members too. Everyone wants to feel noticed and welcomed.

If visitors are not warmly welcomed, they may not come back. That may lose souls for God's kingdom because they won't see a God of love if His people don't show love. This is true of members too. If they aren't warmed by fellowship and friendship, they will eventually drift away and be lost.

Stress the positive

Answer any questions about the church, the pastor, the worship service, and so on with politeness and a positive tone. (Congregation members may also have questions.) For example:

"Our pastor is new, but we love him already. I'm sure you will too."

"I know you will enjoy the service; you can follow it in your worship folder." (Give the visitor a worship folder or direct him or her to an usher who is handing them out.)

If a visitor is late, greet him or her with a gentle comment such as, "Since our service has started, let me show you to a place near the back." Remember to be gracious to late-coming visitors. They may have gotten lost trying to find the church for the first time.

Watching, Touching, Helping, and Other Knotty Challenges

Watching for a deep need

As you greet or seat visitors, watch for the person who looks rumpled or sad or seems nervous and distracted (when no one is distracting him or her). A visitor may come to church because he or she hopes to find answers to gnawing questions, hope to replace despair, love instead of loneliness—or solutions to any of a host of other sorrows or needs.

If you spot such a visitor, you might ask that person if there's something you or the pastor can do for him or her. If you are not comfortable with that, or there is no time for a big question like that, alert the ushers to the person. The ushers may have more time to ask about the person's problem, or, if the person is visibly distraught, at least they can keep an eye on the person during worship.

Be certain that person fills out a visitor card or writes a full name, address, and phone number in the guest book. After the service, alert the pastor to the potential problem so that he can follow up with a phone call or a visit.

Little efforts like this can give the Holy Spirit the opportunity to reach the souls He dearly loves.

Note: Members may also give greeters clues about a need they have. These should also be passed along to the pastor for follow-up.

How much help should you give?

Offering to help never hurts. The person can always turn you down. Inform the ushers of any special need you discover—such as a physical disability.

Ask, "Would you like to sit with a member who can help you follow the worship service?" Have a few members ready ahead of time to serve as guides through the order of worship. Tell the usher to seat the person with one of the worship-service guides and to introduce them to each other, if possible.

If the visitor is elderly, ask, "Would you like to have a large-print bulletin/order of service and a large-print hymnal?" Also, "Would you like me to seat you near the front where you will be able to see and hear everything?"

If the person obviously cannot see or cannot hear, ask, "How can I help you to participate in the service?" Alert ushers to those who might need special help during the service. The ushers can help the person walk to the communion rail or ascend/descend steps, or can alert the pastor to bring the elements to a disabled or elderly person who stays in the pew.

Should you touch people?

One Sunday, Mrs. A. R. visits your church. She is holding a baby in a car-seat cradle and pulling a toddler along by the hand. She is not smiling; she looks apprehensive. What might you do and say to her?

You pat the baby's cheek and lift the toddler to your arms. Mrs. A. R. does not look pleased. Shouldn't she be complimented that you acknowledged her children?

Whether to touch people is a personal matter for each greeter to decide. If it can be done comfortably, do it. Shake hands (or at least offer your hand) or touch a shoulder. Touching someone keeps his or her attention on you; so will meeting their eyes as you talk or listen to him or her.

Luke 6:19 tells us that "the people all tried to touch Him [Jesus], because power was coming from Him and healing them all." Jesus put His hands on children and adults. He even touched lepers to heal them.

Touch has power; people need it to feel loved and cared for. People who are ill have a better chance of recovering if they are touched repeatedly. Children who grow up without being touched often become emotionally disturbed or angry.

The apostle Paul tells the Christians he writes to in several of his epistles that they should "greet each other with a holy kiss."

In our society, the "holy kiss" might be an embarrassing greeting. However, a hug is not out of the question. Tune in to how the person you greet is responding to you. Let the member or visitor's behavior guide you in how (or if) you touch him or her.

Note: Don't touch babies or small children, especially on the face. It spreads germs to the little ones, especially if you have shaken many hands.

Also, after you finish greeting people by shaking hands, *wash your hands with soap and hot water before you do anything else.* It will protect you from someone's cold or flu germs transferred from their hands to yours in a handshake.

Talk or think about the following situations a greeter might face. As a greeter, in which instances might touch be appropriate or inappropriate? What kind of touch could you use?

- An elderly parent of a member comes to church with him or her.

- A teenage boy you haven't met walks past you with his hands in his pockets.

- A pregnant woman—a visitor—comes by you.

- A father escorting two toddlers by the hands passes you as he tries to hang on to both of them.

Children in the worship service?

While a nursery is necessary for some parents with small children, it isn't for everyone. Sometimes children don't want to be separated from their parents—especially not the first time they visit a church. Some parents prefer to have their children go to church with them. Should greeters/ushers encourage parents to take their children along to the worship service?

This is a controversial question—among ministers especially; there's no easy answer. One side of the debate says: How will children learn to sit quietly in church and participate in the order of worship unless they attend church? Should church time become "play in the nursery" time? The other side argues that children distract parents, other worshipers, and the pastor. Which side do you agree with? Express why you think so. Discuss or consider both sides of the debate.

At what point should children be taken out of church? Should an usher suggest strongly to parents that they should remove the child from the worship service and go to the nursery? Each congregation has a different child-tolerance level—as does every pastor or worship leader. How can you find out what your congregation and pastor's tolerance level is for children?

A simpler problem to solve is this: If a child goes to a worship service, that child should sit with parents or other adults, not alone or in unattended groups. Church is where children learn how to praise God, hear His Word, pray, and even attend the Lord's Supper. In some churches, children go to the communion rail with their parents. Each child receives a blessing from the pastor. Is this done in your congregation? If not, how can you begin this practice?

Jesus said, "Let the little children come to Me, and do not hinder them, for the kingdom of heaven belongs to such as these" (Matthew 19:14). In the light of this passage, should children be allowed to attend worship services? What reasons are there for allowing even small children to attend worship services? What "rules" should be enforced if small children are permitted to attend?

One way churches reach out to the community is through a preschool program. Separate preschool classes may be offered for 3- and 4-year-olds, a "kids day out" program for 2-year-olds, and day care for children up to age 5. Since the children learn Bible stories and Jesus songs in school, they become the evangelistic missionaries to their parents. Many families may become members of the church because of the preschool's influence. How might a program like this help with the problem of children going to regular Sunday worship?

Going the Extra Mile for Visitors— and for Yourself

Read the bulletin!

If you are the greeter or usher on duty, spend a few minutes before the service acquainting yourself with the day's bulletin. For example: Is there a special order of service today? If there is a guest preacher, what is his name and where is he from? What activities are planned for today and throughout the week? Are there small-group Bible classes during the week? When does the youth group meet?

If you know these important small details, you are able to give visitors information they can use.

Participate in the service!

In one congregation, a man volunteers to usher as often as possible. But his motives are suspect. As an usher, he can stay in the narthex outside of the nave, move about freely, go outdoors and smoke, or discuss the latest sports scores with another usher. His wife attends worship in the nave alone most of the time.

Unfortunately, ushers and greeters sometimes use their outside-of-the-nave position to excuse them from being a member of the worshiping congregation.

There's no rule that says ushers and greeters need not participate in the worship service. Quite the contrary! Each usher and greeter should have a hymnal and a worship folder. About 10 minutes into the service, the greeters may be seated in the nave. The ushers will take over from that point.

However, that doesn't mean the ushers stop worshiping. Besides being robbed of the praise and prayer experience, nonparticipating ushers are not good models to the worshiping congregation.

Ushers can participate in the service and also keep watch over the worshipers. In fact, they should be at their post (doorway/aisle) and visible to the people. That way, the ushers are giving an example of worship. And they are letting the people and the pastor know there is help standing by if they need it. (Note: Consider having some kind of quiet intercom system between the head usher and the pastor, in case the pastor needs help with something.)

The idea is for the ushers to be so aware and attentive that problems are solved quickly and quietly.

For example, suppose an elderly worshiper slumps onto the pew during the worship service. The ushers should be so quick to see the distressed person that three or four of them are at the scene in seconds. The ill person can be carried out or walked out, depending on his or her condition. If the church is large, the other worshipers might hardly notice.

Is this an idealized scenario or can ushers really keep a service running with hardly a ripple, even if there is a serious emergency?

Here is one example: During a service, a woman was quickly located by the attentive usher and quietly escorted out when her mother, who lived at a nursing home, unexpectedly died. The usher also informed the pastor by handing him a note at an appropriate moment so he could include the woman and her family in the prayers. There was no interruption in the worship.

You may be able to tell stories of attentive ushers who solved emergencies during a worship service without interrupting the flow of things.

Most of the time, the worship service will go without a hitch. But attentive ushers are ready to spring into action as needed.

Involve the pastor in welcoming visitors

If the pastor greets people before or after services, be sure you introduce each visitor to him by name. Tell the pastor something about a visitor if possible—such as which member brought him or her. It will help the pastor place the person.

Perhaps each greeter could be responsible for a portion of the visitors so that one person doesn't have to remember all the visitors' names.

If it is a communion service, ask visitors if they wish to attend the Lord's Supper. Direct those who say they do to the pastor before the service. He can determine best who is prepared to attend.

And who knows who might be one of your visitors: "Keep on loving each other as brothers. Do not forget to entertain strangers, for by so doing some people have entertained angels without knowing it" (Hebrews 13:1–2). Abraham did (Genesis 18) and others in the Bible did too. Do you believe this might happen today?

Follow-up

As said before, try to make a second contact after the service: "It was so nice to have you visit, Mr. Smith. Please visit us again soon."

Introduce the guest to another member—especially if there is a fellowship hour following the service. The member can escort the guest to the fellowship hall. Some congregations have set up a "take a visitor home to dinner" program as a way to follow up a guest's initial visit.

The follow-up call

Give visitor cards/information to the evangelism committee, the pastor, or whoever makes a follow-up call to visitors. Make the call within the week. If the people are not home, persist with calls until you do reach someone.

If it's obvious that the visitor was part of the extended family of a member, follow up through the member who brought the visitor. It may well be that Grandma and Grandpa were here just for a grandchild's Baptism and have their own church home. Another way to identify extended-family visitors is to have a line on the visitor card that allows them to write whom they came with.

Sheep stealing?

The visitor cards also should have a line or two where visitors can make note of their home church. If, in the follow-up call, you discover they are members of another church or even another Christian denomination, thank them again for visiting your church. However, it is probably best to let the follow-up drop at that point. The purpose of follow-up is to offer the ministry of your congregation to those who do not have a church home, not to steal sheep from another pasture.

II. USHERS

Introduction: What Is an Usher?

In one sense, you could say that John the Baptist was an usher. "In those days John the Baptist came, preaching in the Desert of Judea and saying, 'Repent, for the kingdom of heaven is near.' This is He who was spoken of through the prophet Isaiah: 'A voice of one calling in the desert, "Prepare the way for the Lord, make straight paths for Him" ' " (Matthew 3:1–3).

John the Baptist came before Jesus and prepared the way for Him. One definition of *usher* is "to precede as a forerunner." You might say you, in the role of usher, precede the worshipers to prepare the church building or to prepare the way to worship for those who come to church.

Another definition of *usher* is "an officer who walks before a person of rank." Have you ever attended a graduation where someone preceded the professors or teachers to their places in the auditorium? The person who "marshals" the people of rank or distinction is "ushering" them.

You can even say that, as an usher at church, you "marshal" or "usher" people into the presence of Christ—who is of the highest rank: King of kings and Lord of lords. When you usher people into a church's nave, you lead them into the presence of God—for the church is God's house.

Ushers as hosts

Even more than the greeters, the ushers are the hosts for the worship service. Whether an usher wants to, he or she represents the entire congregation. The hospitality of the usher tells the visitors what kind of hospitality the rest of the congregation will show to them.

We will consider each of the following questions. You might wish to write a preliminary answer and then refer back to this page after you finish this part of the booklet.

How can you put visitors at ease? _____

_____

How do you help them participate fully in the worship service? Is handing them a bulletin enough?

_____

_____

What problems with visitors are most likely to develop? How do/will you solve the problems?

_____

_____

Treat every visitor as if he or she were a visiting angel (Hebrews 13:1–2). How would you treat such a visiting angel? _____

_____

Which public servant are you most like when you serve as an usher? Explain your choice.
- A police officer?
- A waiter/waitress?
- A bellhop?

_____

_____

What do visitors want?

Visitors have four basic needs:
- they need to feel *welcome;*
- they need to feel *comfortable;*
- they need to feel *listened to;* and
- they need to feel *important.*

The ushering staff needs to serve the church visitors' needs with genuine concern for the satisfaction of every individual visitor.

1. Make visitors feel *welcome,* smile, shake their hands, ask their names, etc. Especially in their first few

tentative moments in a new church, make them feel very glad they came.

2. Make visitors feel *comfortable,* show genuine interest in them, but don't overdo it. Answer questions and offer help with anything they need. Seat them where they can see and hear well, and, if possible, near a member who can help them follow the service.

3. Make visitors feel *"listened to,"* pay careful attention to whatever they say to you: their names, any help they need (where rest rooms are, for example), and where they would feel most comfortable when sitting in the nave.

4. Make visitors feel *important,* use their names when speaking to them. Go the extra mile for them, even if it means an inconvenience for you. Anticipate their needs as much as possible, without interfering with their comfort or their worship.

Discuss the four needs of a visitor explained above. Do you agree with these? What other needs might visitors have? _____

_____

_____

The duties of an usher can be done enthusiastically or mechanically—as dull chores. It's a matter of attitude, as you read in the first section of this booklet. Let's spend a few minutes learning how God wants you to approach your ushering role.

Keeping everybody happy

It's impossible! Keeping visitors, members, pastor, greeters, and fellow ushers all happy is impossible.

For example, some may want all noisy children to be immediately removed from the service. The child's parents may have a much higher tolerance of their child's noise level. As usher, whom do you please?

_____

In most cases, the worship service must continue uninterrupted as much as possible. The worshipers are in the presence of God and are praising, praying to and listening to Him through the pastor, the liturgy, the prayers, the Bible readings, and the hymns.

In the event that a child becomes noisy, for example, give the parents a little time to settle the child down. If the noise continues, go to the parent who is taking care of the child and whisper (if possible) something like, "May I show you to the nursery?" If the parent refuses and the noise continues and is obviously disturbing worshipers, you must insist on the parent removing the disruptive child from the service.

No matter how hard you work, there will be problems during worship. The quiet of the worship service will be interrupted, most of the time, by something—perhaps just briefly. Don't become upset by the interruptions. Work quickly and as quietly as possible to take care of the interruptions and let the service continue. You will do best if you face each problem with a calm command of the situation. What interruptions might you face—or have you faced—that require immediate attention? (We will spend more time on this under "Emergencies.")

A story about interruptions in worship services concerns a very excellent organist and choir director who seemed able to concentrate on the music in church without being distracted by anything. When asked how he concentrated so successfully, he said, "I had excellent training in ignoring what was going on around me in church. During World War II, when I was in an Anglican cathedral boys' choir, we were told over and over, 'No matter what happens, don't stop the worship.' We sang through air-raid sirens, the sound of airplanes flying over, the jolt of bombs exploding nearby, the screaming sirens of emergency vehicles. The music and the worship never stopped. Nothing could ever equal that; I can concentrate on the music through anything!"

Attitude: Why Is It So Important?

God needs you to "shine like stars"

Read Philippians 2:14–16a. Apply this passage to the role of usher, one verse at a time.

Verse 14: "Do everything without complaining or arguing." _____

_____

But, what about having to pass out hymnals? They are heavy! Or, what about running up and down the balcony stairs to count people and collect offerings? Surely, if you, as an usher, *do* the difficult things, does it matter that you complain about it a little?

Verse 15: "so that you may become blameless and pure, children of God without fault in a crooked and depraved generation, in which you shine like stars in the universe." _____

_____

Do you really need to "shine like stars"? Not only does God want you to have a servant attitude about your ushering duties (see paragraphs in section 1 on the servant attitude under "God's Word speaks on attitude"), He wants you to be perfect and to "shine" so that visitors and members see you as a person who is a shining example for them. How can you accomplish this expectation?

_____

_____

Also read Matthew 5:16. How does what Jesus says here sound like what you read in Philippians 2?

_____

_____

Or, do you think that God is not addressing these passages to you as an usher?

Verse 16a: "as you hold out [or hold onto] the word of life." _____

_____

That's the pastor's job, isn't it? How does this part of the passage speak to you as an usher?

_____

_____

_____

People catch what you have

This isn't about germs. It's about enthusiasm for the worship services, the pastor, the people, the Word, the Sacraments—and everything connected with God's house, the church. The visitors and members will catch your mood and attitude about the church—be it negative or positive—whether you actually say something to them or not. What is going on in your mind and heart will show on your face.

Psalm 27:4 describes the attitude you want to reflect to worshipers about the church: "One thing I ask of the LORD, this is what I seek: that I may dwell in the house of the LORD all the days of my life, to gaze upon the beauty of the LORD and to seek Him in His temple."

Appearance Can Be Everything

Christians should not judge people on first impressions, but we do anyway. Since you, as an usher, may be the first person in a congregation that visitors encounter and talk to, your image is vital.

Look your best!

When you are to be an usher at a particular service, be clean and neat. Wear clothing that does not attract attention but is appropriate to solemn worship.

Be on time (at least 20 minutes before the service

begins). Follow instructions from the head usher and accept the place/aisle/task assigned to you.

Wear a name badge. Your name should be legible from a distance so that visitors can call *you* by name when you call *them* by name. Sometimes the ushers are identified by a boutonniere or a pocket badge. Be sure you wear one.

How to show God's love

St. Paul gives a capsule summary of how to be an example of Christ's love to others:

> Love must be sincere. Hate what is evil; cling to what is good. Be devoted to one another in brotherly love. Honor one another above yourselves. Never be lacking in zeal, but keep your spiritual fervor, serving the Lord. Be joyful in hope, patient in affliction, faithful in prayer. Share with God's people who are in need. Practice hospitality.
>
> (Romans 12:9–13)

Which phrases in the above passage apply to the kind of loving service you give as an usher? Write them below and discuss how you can incorporate those qualities and actions in your ushering—and in the rest of your Christian life as well.

_____

_____

_____

_____

Turn what you wrote above into a prayer to God to make you the kind of usher that will please Him and that will bring visitors to Christ.

The ushering team

Though the head usher is responsible for all that must be done in the church building before, during, and after a service, he need not perform all the duties himself. He should delegate the many duties to the people on his ushering team and trust his team to get the job done.

Though they are a team ministry, ushers relate to individuals one at a time. The usher acknowledges, guides, helps, comforts, etc., each of the visitors and other worshipers individually.

By dealing with people individually, the ushering team creates a quiet, reverent place to worship. The ushering team's main goal at each worship service is to create and maintain that quiet atmosphere.

Important Information and Duties

What's in the closet?

In the ushers' closet or cabinet should be supplies that might be needed during a service:

- emergency phone numbers posted on the door, unless you have 911 service available
- a candlelighter and a small bell-shaped candle snuffer; and a supply of matches
- fire extinguisher
- a working intercom (connected with both pastor and organist), if possible
- offering plates
- a lost-and-found collection box
- a first-aid kit
- flashlights and penlights that work; extra batteries
- "reserved" markers for reserving pews
- sharpened pencils
- extra visitor cards
- extra name tags and visitor-identification badges
- paper towels (you never know what might end up on the carpet!)

- several bags of Emesis Vomit Absorbent or similar compound
- paper cups (for water)
- box of facial tissues
- tracts about your church
- on the wall near the closet: light switches/dimmers and spotlight controls for the nave, sanctuary, altar, pulpit, narthex (area just before entering the sanctuary), etc. All ushers should be taught how to control the lights.

Is anything missing from this list of supplies that might be needed during worship at your church? If so, add it here:

- _____
- _____
- _____

Duties and responsibilities of ushers

1. Act as greeters if there are none—if your congregation doesn't have greeters or if the greeters fail to show up for their assigned worship service.

Just as with the greeters, find a substitute for yourself if you cannot usher at a service assigned to you.

2. Hand out bulletins/worship folders/etc., and provide a word of explanation if needed—especially if the service moves back and forth from worship folder to hymnal.

Be sure there are a few large-print bulletins available to offer to the elderly or visually impaired.

3. Make sure the pastor is "wired for sound." Many congregations have a clip-on microphone with a battery pack for the pastor to wear so he can move around and still be heard. Keeping the pastor's voice amplified is the responsibility of the ushers—or whomever is assigned to that duty.

4. Be attentive to people and pastor every moment in case of a need or an emergency. It was an alert usher who, with a handy fire extinguisher, put out the flames he saw starting in the Christmas decorations in the sanctuary behind the pastor. Without the usher's instant response, the entire building could have burned. There might even have been loss of life.

5. Before the service

- Unlock the doors;
- Turn on the lights;
- Open the windows (as needed);
- Adjust the heating/air-conditioning system;
- Turn on the sound system and give the pastor the clip-on microphone and battery pack.

6. Mark any reserved seating (such as back rows for parents with small children) and guide those who are to sit there to seats in that section.

7. When greeting visitors, find out each person's name and seating preference. Guide them to a seat as near as possible to the place they requested or ask if they will agree to a compromise. Encourage people to sit toward the front of the nave. However, don't put visitors in the front row. If they are first-time visitors, they cannot be expected to know when to stand or to otherwise lead the congregation.

8. Be sensitive to those with disabilities and assist those who need special help: hard-of-hearing or deaf, blind, elderly, in wheelchairs, etc.

9. Quiet the people in the narthex outside the nave when the worship service begins. Often, people in the narthex are visiting and are not aware that the service has started. The noise can be very distracting to those who want to focus on the worship service.

10. Turn on the speaker in the nursery so the caretakers can hear the worship service. (If you don't have a speaker in the nursery, get one. It is a way for caretak-

ers to participate in the service and for small children to hear what the service sounds like.)

11. Count the worshipers as inconspicuously as possible, if your congregation keeps track of the number of worshipers in each service.

Have extra chairs ready to set up in your overflow area as needed. Extra chairs will especially be needed for services such as confirmation, when extended families attend your church.

12. Gather the offering; take it to the altar; know where and how long to stand before the altar.

13. Assist with Holy Communion. Direct the worshipers to the front of the nave smoothly and quickly, without embarrassing any of those who commune. Know how many worshipers may process to the communion rail for one table, and count how many people you direct to the front for each table. Know the route for those who commune to process up to the communion rail and then back to their seats without interfering with the next table of people.

Direct the worshipers as smoothly and quietly as possible. Do it with gestures and body language rather than talking, if you can.

Help those with any difficulties. (You may even be constrained to watch or hold a small child, if your congregation doesn't allow children to accompany their parents to the communion rail.) Help the elderly or physically disabled up and down steps.

Gather communion registration cards.

Some churches use an usher to help the pastor distribute the bread or wine. The need for a helper in the sanctuary should be determined by the ruling body of the congregation. The congregation may want to supply the usher/elder communion helpers with a robe similar to the pastor's. When assisting with Holy Communion, rehearse with the pastor and do as he directs.

14. Assist with Holy Baptism. An usher may be asked to help the pastor with a Baptism. But the usher's main duties for a Baptism during the service

are: Before the service begins, remove any covering over the baptismal font and fill the font with water. Some congregations have a special pitcher, a ewer, that is used to fill the baptismal font with water. Seat the baptismal family near the baptismal font.

Usher the parents and sponsors to the font at the proper time. Hold the Baptism certificate and the towel until needed, and hold the missal (altar book) for the pastor so his hands are free. From the altar candles, light the baptismal candle given to the parents, if that is customary. Usher the family back to their seats when the Baptism is over.

15. Miscellaneous duties:

- Set out the guest book and pen;
- Direct guests to sign visitor cards;
- Put the offering plates in place;
- Post hymn numbers;
- If ushers wear pocket badges, make sure the color matches the liturgical color of the paraments on the altar.
- Light the altar candles if there is no acolyte;
- Check emergency supplies (such as a first-aid kit and several bags of Emesis Vomit Absorbent);
- Check rest rooms before, during (if possible), and after services to make sure they are clean and have not become a playground for children;
- Relay messages to the pastor during the service, if needed;
- Ring the church bell, if your church has one; this may be done by the organist;
- Order supplies (cards, pencils, etc.) for use during the worship services.

16. Collect items from exiting worshipers at the nave doors: hymnals, special offerings, filled-out cards, etc. Distribute any handouts as the people leave.

17. After the service, extinguish candles, turn off lights, close windows (as needed), turn down/off the heating/air-conditioning system, turn off the sound system, and lock doors. Make sure everything is ready for the next service—whether in an hour or in a week.

Ushers also straighten up the nave after the service: Put hymnals, Bibles, visitor cards, pencils, etc., in their proper places; collect service bulletins that were left on the pews and discard them (or place in church office to be sent to shut-in members); collect items left by worshipers and either make them available or put them in the church's lost-and-found. It would be helpful to list in the next Sunday's bulletin the lost items so people can claim them.

18. Collect attendance/visitor cards and give them to the pastor, the church secretary, the evangelism committee, or whoever follows up on visitors.

If you can think of any more duties and responsibilities of ushers, especially those unique to your church building or worship service or pastor, write them below.

19. _____

20. _____

21. _____

22. Remember, you are the congregation's representative to visitors. Are visitors going to leave impressed with the warmth and friendliness of the congregation or with the cold aloofness of the people? Are they going to leave thinking well of God's people or not? It is a solemn responsibility that takes a joyful face.

Occasional services

Funerals: Since these may be scheduled at any time, the head usher should be sure that one or two ushers can be available. Retired people are usually happy to serve. (In fact, when recruiting ushers from the membership, do not overlook the over-65 members of your congregation who may be just waiting to be asked to help.)

At a funeral, be warm but subdued with your greetings. A smile is always appropriate. Keep the people quiet before and during the service.

Usher the family members into and out of the nave. You, the representative of the church, rather than the employees of the undertaking establishment, should escort the family members. Assist with moving the casket as needed.

Don't be too quick to clean up after the service is over. Let mourners take their time.

Weddings: The head usher should have one or two experienced ushers in the narthex to help the one-time ushers (friends and relatives of the bride and groom) to carry out the ushering duties. What the one-time ushers don't or cannot do, the regular ushers should do.

There will be many guests in your church for a wedding. Be sure they are greeted, directed, and helped— much as they would be if they came on Sunday morning.

Unless it is done by the one-time ushers, usher in the families of the bride and the groom. The mother of the bride and of the groom (and the grandmothers) should be escorted alone on the usher's arm.

The bride's and groom's families usually sit on opposite sides near the front. You may also have to usher the family members out again after the ceremony.

Ushers should ask each person if he or she would like to sit on the bride's side or the groom's side. Seat all the guests on the side they request, if possible. Allow ladies to hold your arm as you escort them to a place in the nave.

Regular ushers should also direct the acolytes or light the candles themselves. There may be more candles than in a regular service. Light them as quickly as possible.

As part of the after-service cleanup, you may have to sweep up the rice on the church's outside steps.

Other services: Some congregations have weekday evening services during Advent (the four weeks before Christmas) and Lent (the six weeks before Easter). Ushers should be on duty at all services.

Any other services (Good Friday, Ascension Day, Christmas Eve, for example) should be planned weeks in advance so that there will be ushers on hand and so that they will know what to do if the service is different from a usual Sunday service.

Emergencies

Ushers will have to face emergencies during worship services. Some are important and some insignificant.

How would you deal with each of the following "emergencies"? Each congregation and pastor has a different tolerance level for disturbances. Answer the following to fit your situation.

1. Latecomer (Do not allow latecomers to be seated in the nave during a Bible reading or prayer.)

———————————————————————————

2. Offering plate dropped (If it is between the pews, the people sitting there will have to help pick up the coins, bills, and envelopes.) ————————————

———————————————————————————

3. Slow-moving exit of worshipers (Direct some to side aisles.) ————————————————————

———————————————————————————

4. Teenagers catching up on everything by incessantly whispering to each other. (A simple finger-across-the-lips gesture might be enough.) ————————————

———————————————————————————

5. Baby who is crying or is otherwise noisy. (If the child is disturbing worshipers or the pastor, the parent

should take him/her out.) _____

_____

_____

6. Child vomits. (The parent should take the child out of the service immediately, but the usher might get cleanup duty. Sprinkle some Emesis Vomit Absorbent or similar compound on it. This deodorizes it and makes the cleanup easier.) _____

_____

_____

7. Child leaves the service. (What you do depends on the tolerance level of the congregation and the pastor.) _____

_____

8. Adult leaves the service. (You can assume it is for a good reason. Ask if you can help if the person seems ill.) _____

_____

9. Candle on the altar goes out. (Leave it out.)

_____

_____

10. Electricity goes off. (Depends on the availability of daylight and whether heat or air-conditioning is needed. Wait a few minutes; it might come back on.)

_____

_____

_____

11. Someone faints. (Get to the person fast and take help along.) _____

_____

12. Someone (possibly drunk) talks loudly and interrupts the service. (Get to the person fast and take help along.) _____

_____

Add some of your own emergencies. Be sure to include solutions to the problems.

13. _____

14. _____

15. _____

Checklist for ushers

From the list of the duties and responsibilities of an usher, the usher staff should work out a checklist for your church's ushers for each service. With a checklist to mark off each duty as it is accomplished, nothing will be skipped and any embarrassment will be avoided.

The checklist should be filled out by the head usher or by one usher on duty at each service.

The indispensable usher

As you have learned, it is nearly impossible to run a church service "decently and in order" without the silent, inconspicuous service of good ushers. To keep this "we can't do it without you" idea in perspective, we quote the apostle Paul:

> Whatever you do, do it all for the glory of God. Do not cause anyone to stumble, whether Jews, Greeks or the church of God—even as I try to please everybody in every way. For I am not seeking my own good but the good of many, so that they may be saved.

> (1 Corinthians 10:31b–33)

Soli Deo Gloria!